RESIDENTIAL ARCHITECTURE:
LIVING PLACES

Published by
The
Ashley
Group

First published in the United State of America in 2002 by
The Ashley Group
1350 East Touhy Ave.
Des Plaines, IL 60018
847.390.2882; 847.390.2902 FAX

Design consultation by Shook Design
Written by Lynne Schreiber

1668 Telegraph Road, Suite 350
Bloomfield Hills, MI 48302
248.335.8888; 248.335.0944 FAX

www.DTArchitects.com

Library of Congress Cataloguing-in-Publication Data
Residential Architecture: Living Places
p. cm.
Includes bibliographical references.
ISBN1588620883

Tringali, Dominick
1. Architecture, Modern - 20th century - United States. I. Tringali,
Dominick.
2002
720 '02-dc 20
CIP 2001012345

Front cover: Tessmar Residence; Rochester Hills, Michigan;
               Completed 1998; S. Benjamin, Photographer

Back cover: Brandon Residence; Grand Rapids, Michigan;
               Completed 1997; Michael Neumann, Photographer

Printed in Hong Kong

ISBN: 1-58862-088-3

First Edition

Residential Architecture:
Living Places

Table of Contents

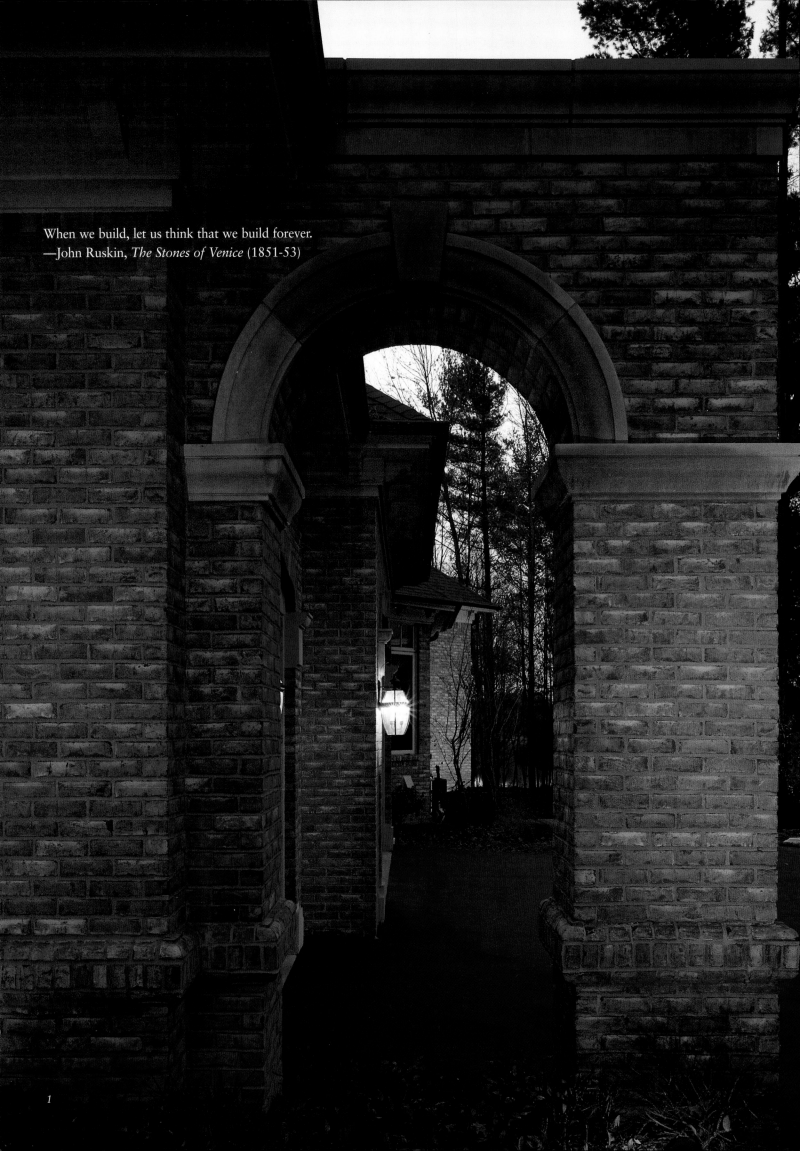

When we build, let us think that we build forever.
—John Ruskin, *The Stones of Venice* (1851-53)

From The Beginning

1. *Boskovich Residence, Brighton Township, Michigan.*
2. *St. Peter's Cathedral (1987). Sketch by Dominick.*
3. *Roman Forum (1980). Watercolor by Dominick.*

Architect Eliel Saarinen was once quoted in *Time Magazine* as saying one should always design a thing by considering it in its larger context—a chair in a room, a room in a house, a house in an environment, an environment in a city plan.

Half a century later, it is those words exactly that are echoed in the designs of Michigan architect Dominick Tringali, a well-known residential designer who emphasizes the need to create structures that harmonize with lifestyles and with the natural environment.

Careful attention to the architectural masters that came before him has allowed Dominick Tringali to evolve into the residential architect that he is today.

As a young architectural student, Dominick devoured the resources before him, looking for lessons in the buildings of his mentors. He became an avid follower of famed architects Robert Stern and Hugh Newell Jacobsen. Both created a wide variety of structures, always basing their designs on the enduring values of classicism. Stern is viewed as one of the greatest influences in the Post-Modernism movement, rooting his designs in culture and arguing for a study of history to complement architecture.

Yet, the oldest lessons determined the style and character of Dominick's work. His first architecturally defining moment came in Europe in the mid-1980s. Walking the streets of Rome, he gazed at and studied the angles of buildings that had stood watch for many centuries, through wars and conquests. He stood humbled in the center of the Colosseum. "This is the spot where Caesar stood," the tour guide explained, and Dominick stepped into the shoes of the great, historical leader. He gazed out at the expanse of the architectural relic. Having finished his studies and begun work in the field, Dominick recalls that moment crystal-lizing all that he had learned.

"I stood in a different time frame, staring at the ingenuity of the Roman era," he said. "The tour guide was talking about the symbolism that the architecture created for the Roman Empire. I knew then that I wanted to do the right things to make my creations stand the test of time."

Part of Dominick's strength lay in his ability to learn from various greats and meld the best of their theories and practices into his own unique mix. He found inspiration in the work of Canadian architect Arthur Erickson, an organic residential

2

3

architect who builds in harmony with nature. Erickson's signature style incorporates urban design with imaginative landscape, fully integrating trees, water, and other site-specific foliage. To that end, Dominick believes in letting the site and its surrounding environment determine the way a house should progress. Both the client's input and the site layout concur to determine the technique Dominick's firm—Dominick Tringali Architects—will use on a given project. The ultimate creation is the result of ongoing dialogue among the design team and the client.

Yet, it was Christopher Alexander who most inspired Dominick's humanistic approach to his craft. "Alexander promotes architecture that nurtures human life," he said. "That is a powerful idea, and one on which our firm has always been based. We develop lifestyles. We design houses on a humanistic scale."

Not long ago, Dominick returned to Europe to study the architecturally significant sites of England. Ten years after his initial realizations in Rome, he stood in the British town of Bath, watching Alexander's philosophy of humanism and scale come to life.

The streets were narrow; despite centuries of improvements, people still had priority over automobiles. He watched the roads wind and noticed the way the architecture fit into the landscape, the way people fit into the architecture. Everything about that visit impressed him. Centuries-old architecture, while becoming refined over time, still felt proportional to modern-day needs.

"It felt good being in the piazzas and courtyards. That visit made me realize that we need to build more communities, more towns. Homes need to have the same feeling. We don't really need big vaulted ceilings and high spaces—we need spaces that relate to the way we live."

He returned to the States and reread Alexander's book, *Pattern Language*, gaining a whole new perspective decades into his career. He routinely reflects on Alexander's drive to create buildings with richness, resonance, and life—qualities most often found in older buildings. Without imitating, but rather creating new structures with a mixture of styles, Dominick follows Alexander's analysis of healthy communities that came to be known as the New Urbanism. Alexander experiments with ways to create forms in harmony with their environment, sometimes applying scientific principles to planning theory.[1]

5

6

It is Alexander who insists that architecture must evolve on the site rather than on paper, a philosophy that Dominick embraces wholeheartedly. He has always sought to work within the laws of nature that demand organic structures in a harmony of elements.

Today, despite an ever-increasing number of trained architects, the residential market has become less effective in creating environments where people feel comfortable, whole, and happy.[2]

"Home is a place of security within an insecure world, a place of certainty within doubt, a familiar place in a strange world, a sacred place in a profane world. It is a place of autonomy and power in an increasingly heteronomous world where others make the rules.
—Kimberly Dovey, "Home and Homelessness," in *Home Environments, Human Behavior and Environment, Advances in Theory and Research*

Given the task of creating such a setting, he must listen carefully to his clients and trust his architectural instincts. He listens to the land, too. One of Dominick's greatest assets is his ability to look at the entire picture when creating a structure— it's always about bringing society together in a fusion of lifestyle, environment, and beauty, never a lone building, face to the wind.

"We rarely do sculptural architecture, architecture that on its own merit and basis has meaning but may be out of context with the neighborhood. We do contextual architecture. We fit a dwelling into the surrounding neighborhood. Everything must be harmonious and blend."

7

8

9

10

7. *An example of early Contemporary style designed in the 1980s.*

8. *The early 1980s was also a time in which Dominick experimented in classic, traditional tudor styles.*

9. *Built in the mid 1980s, this home developed into a more Traditional style, bringing back balance of form, symmetrical elevations, and gable and hip roofs. This was the beginning of Dominick Tringali's in-depth approach to create architecture that stands the test of time.*

10. *In the late 1980s, a demand for traditional, more historic homes led to the design and development of this type of classic English style which Dominick began to refine.*

11. *An LTA-era home, whose interior reflects the familiar floor plans of the 1980s—open, with abundant light, spaces in which people wanted to live. This era of LTA architecture featured quoined corners, balconies, courtyards, and detailed fireplaces.*

12-14. *In the experimental phase of his career, Dominick Tringali tried his hand at Prairie Style (bottom), California Modern Contemporary (middle), and French Traditional (top). Each stylistic foray emphasized the need for the principles of balance and form to prevail, regardless of architectural style.*

12

13

14

Perfect harmony made Dominick Tringali into an architect. Driven by the passion of a hard-working, Italian family, Dominick's dreams were molded by the closeness engendered by an outspoken, ever-present mother and a hard-working father, who was always trying to improve upon the process. Had his family not come from Italy, in fact, he may not have earned the acclaim that he enjoys today. In a manner of perspective, it has always been a family affair. Dominick's drawing talent mirrors his father's pensive inventiveness. An automotive worker all his life, the elder Tringali was always trying to improve on the way he handled any task. Dominick's mother was a typical Italian mom, always there, always outspoken. "My heritage was a strong part of my development and those styles were transposed later in my career," he said.

The only member of his family born in the United States, Dominick took his first trip to Italy when he was five and returned when he was 10 and 15. After the second trip, he knew architecture was where his fortune lay.

He was fascinated by the oldest designs, buildings such as the Colosseum, that not only stood testament to periods of intense history but also weathered the winds of change over centuries. Dominick yearned to learn what it took to create structures that last. Include that with his skill for drawing, and his future was a foregone conclusion.

In high school, Dominick devoted his attention to drawing and drafting, talents that later took him to Lawrence Technological University's architectural program. By then, he had visited Italy four times and even studied there, each visit offering a deeper understanding of the impressive, classic dwellings he stumbled upon.

Finally, the shape of his lifelong goals was taking form. Throughout college, Dominick worked for firms that gave him experience with residential projects, corporate jobs, retail and commercial designs. All the while, he kept coming back to his first love: residential structures. In 1985, he went to work for David Lubin, spending two years as Lubin's head designer, and in 1989, became a partner in what became known as Lubin/ Tringali Associates (LTA). In 1996, the partners parted ways, and Dominick formed Dominick Tringali Associates Architects & Planners. Today, his firm has 30 talented young professionals, individuals who have the drive and instinct to take each project to the architectural limit, while creating structures with staying power.

"I wanted to create a unique company in an inspiring environment," said Dominick. To that end, he designed and built the firm's headquarters, borrowing favorite materials and techniques from his residential forays to create an office with urban appeal and the familiar feel of home.

Today, the firm specializes in all forms of residential architecture, with three main focuses:

■ Luxury custom homes – unique, large residences that vary in size from 6,000 to 25,000 sq. ft.,

■ Mid-range custom homes – structures ranging from 2,500 to 5,000 sq. ft., with construction costs ranging from $800,000 to over $1 million, and

■ Community designs – entire communities, from downtown hubs to livable homes in peaceful environments, all within a context of each other.

Combining the talents of a solid group of individuals, including two vice presidents who have worked with him for nearly two decades, Dominick wants to create a firm that surpasses what any single person can do alone in the architectural world. The team is cohesive. They gather at times on weekends for architectural tours and lessons. Sometimes, the entire staff will read the same book, to think and talk about at length. He recognizes the need to congeal talents into a workable machine that can withstand the pressures and maintain the dynamism of their field.

"We experiment all the time with the latest trends," said Dominick, who likes to marry the best of new styles with the enduring principles of traditional design. While no two homes end up looking the same, each project is guided by the same long-held standards that make good architecture.

There was a time when the team experimented with California Contemporary, Prairie Style, and Post-Modernism. Still, he always came back to what he calls the "tree" that is architecture: "There are many different branches, but the trunk stays the same."

Drawing on his early 1980s experiences with contemporary structures, Dominick mixes the flavor of contemporary and traditional architecture to produce a product that is best described as Transitional. (Transitional architecture denotes the merging of one style with another.) Always, he and his team return to what is timeless—buildings that cannot be pegged for a certain architectural time period. They build structures that age well, that grow with time, meshing with the landscape to create an overall aura and sense of synergy that are impossible to separate.

They specialize in "pattern language" that is comfortable to the human scale. The height of columns must be in proportion to man and his place in the setting, for example. This melds well with the firm's overarching philosophy. "We try to bring out values in style," explained Dominick.

"Buildings are symbolic of the wealth, power, and lifestyle of the ages. Residential architecture is nothing less than the foundation of society. It gives us meaning and purpose. It is what we each call home."

Notes
1. "Hall of fame: Christopher Alexander," Bruce D. Snider, Residential Architect, June 2001.
2. sic

15. *This home of an NFL football player and his family is traditional in its exterior of strong, red brick and a dark roof. Inside, the home is open and unique, geared toward the owners' lifestyle—they entertain often, gathering large groups of people into rooms that blend and intermix. The kitchen flows into the prep areas and breakfast nook, and the living and dining spaces meld into one as needed.*

16. *The exterior was designed to incorporate traditional flavor, yet each element has a purpose, like the exterior arcade that leads directly to the indoor pool and back hall.*

15

16

17. *This was the first house with Dominick Tringali's signature that became a classic. Constructed in the early 1990s—in Pinecreek Estates, Brighton, Michigan—it still has the ability to confuse architectural scholars as to the where and when of its creation. It has aged extremely well, the test of good architecture, and Dominick attributes much of that to the European flair of its arcade, ornate brick detail, limestone touches and added dormers. The interior features more wood trim and moldings than his previous designs. The kitchen, nook, and family room combine to form one usable space, and traditional elements like French doors, transom windows, and high ceilings can be found throughout.*

17

18. Foyer with swooping stair and two-story space.

19. The kitchen breakfast area and a small sitting hearth are combined together to create an interactive family space.

An architect's greatest fulfillment is creating a
'client's dream.' — Dominick Tringali

A Spectrum of Homes

1. *Russell Residence, Rochester Hills, Michigan.*
2. *French Manor Estate of 10,000 sq. ft. in Rochester Hills, Michigan.*
3. *English Tudor Eclectic home with trademark stable garage and arcade design.*

In the story of creating, there are obvious highlights along the way that crystallize design ideologies. The residences in this chapter highlight the variety and breadth of Dominick Tringali's work, from French Traditional to Manor Homes and English Tudor designs. The homes in these pages focus on solid, strong brickwork and intricate stone detail, as well as the use of the European arcade, the emphasis of limestone, and the strength of the entry. These mark the beginning of Dominick's career.

Stony Hollow Subdivision
Rochester Hills, Michigan

These creations combine a variety of architectural styles, including Vernacular Historicism, Neo-Traditionism, Modernism, and the personal touches that distinguish Dominick's style and the eclectic lives of his clients. Ultimately, his houses are utterly livable. As respected architect Dennis Wedlick said, "No one lives in an [architectural] statement."[1] Like Wedlick, Dominick urges his clients to take a chance and go with their romantic, adventurous side on one of the most important endeavors of their lives.

2

1. From "Listen and Learn," S. Claire Conroy, Residential Architect, September 2001.

3

Ferber Residence
West Bloomfield, Michigan
1995

Reflecting a Traditional English cottage style, this house invokes a strong sense of European flair, thanks to beveled glass windows and a detailed entryway. A philosophy of rich character and Old World grace is carried through the home, in archways surrounded by cased-out columns, a solid wood floating stairway, soaring ceilings, a marble foyer, and a piano alcove in the backdrop. The goal for this house was to make everything work together in a timeless fashion.

The details and woodworking were initially designed in the first concept sketches and were carried through into the final working drawings. Each vista and focal point was thought out, from the railing details to the foyer marble inlays.

4

5

18

Dumars Residence
Bloomfield Hills, Michigan
1994

This home is as unique as its owners, Joe Dumars, of the NBA's Detroit Pistons, and his wife, Debbie. The initial idea was to create a touch of Europe. Texture creates form, in a stucco exterior with a limestone base. The home begins with a symmetrical, portico entry with ornate window detailings, colonnades and limestone blocking on the base of the walls. In this home, the firm aimed for a sense of presence. "We tried to enhance the entire area by creating a house that would be the focal point from the street," said Dominick.

The house has a lot of length, with a diagonal garage, so it sits well on the large parcel of land. The floor plan spreads out on the lot, making use of the way the land ebbs and flows. Designed for entertaining, the house features a large, two-story gathering room, a limestone fireplace and two stories of glass up the back of the great room. The kitchen is unique, with a dual island and hearth area, as well as a children's play space. This home embodies the open, flowing floor plan of the 1990s, melding with the owners' lifestyle.

7

8

9

10

Ajluni Residence
Bloomfield Hills, Michigan
1996

This Traditional formal manor home has particularly heavy limestone detail around the windows and a warm limestone entryway. The lot called for a house that would intermingle with existing large trees but still have a formal presence to blend with the surrounding neighborhood.

Boskovich Residence
Brighton Township, Michigan
1997

With this residence, Dominick began designing in true Italianate style. A low-pitched roof paired with the formality of the windows and, once again, warm, limestone details. Here, he included courtyards and balustrades out front as well as serious detailing along the windows and brickwork. This home sits on a lake lot in a neighborhood and was designed to accomodate its clients' desires for a floor plan with views to the lake and woods beyond.

11

12

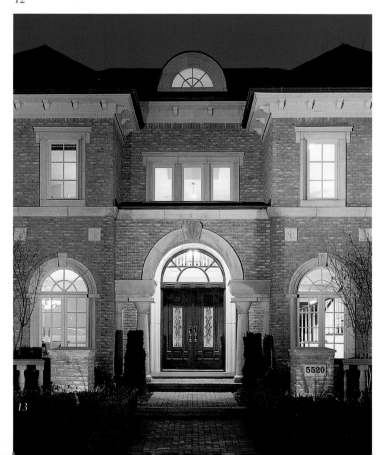

13

Novak Residence
Bingham Farms, Michigan
1996

The stately style of a French Manor home is perfect for a large lot, where it can settle into the sweep of the land as if it were meant to lay down and slumber on the property. This home was designed with a limestone and stucco finish, incorporated French balconies, and featured a carriage house garage with arcade. "We designed this into the lay of the land—a low-lying house with swooping roofs that appeared to come right out of the ground," Dominick explained. Surrounding trees influenced the proportions of the home, which incorporated a first-floor master bedroom suite and low line design to avoid two-story spaces as much as possible. The result was perfect balance and harmony with the land.

14

15

Cohen Residence
West Bloomfield, Michigan
1996

It may be Michigan, but this California Contemporary home features stucco on the facade with trellis detail and a dramatic, vaulted entryway. Dominick took extra precaution when designing the lighting, so it would flow with the architecture. The desired effect was a casual yet dramatic house, blending into the wooded lot on which it sits.

Strickstein Residence
Orchard Lake, Michigan
1998

Perhaps lakefront is apt for a Classic Contemporary, as large pieces of glass maximize the view of the water. Because this lot is narrow, the design of the home had to maximize all water views while working its way around large trees.

Tessmar Residence
Rochester Hills, Michigan
1998

The slope of the land at the edge of a cul de sac determined the placement for this home's turret, entryway and garage. Here, Dominick relied on limestone and brick detail to provide a traditional feel. He also added specialty wood brackets and trim to the facade, which enhances its overall appearance.

16

17

18

19. *Traditional Bungalow style.*
20. *English Tudor porte-cochère.*
21. *Original floor plan sketches for Zalesin residence.*

M. Menuck Residence
Birmingham, Michigan
1997

All of Dominick's skill was used to create this 26 ft. wide design. The home was planned for younger clients, and it features contextual architecture to the maximum degree. The traditional bungalow style needed to blend with the neighborhood and the surrounding 40 ft. wide lots. Dominick used brick, shake and a unique Victorian asphalt roof to elicit the ambience of the era.

Zalesin Residence
Birmingham, Michigan
1996

The grandness of this Tudor home began in the porte-cochère, a dramatic entryway that speaks of affluence and Victorian flavor. Here, it also minimizes the appearance of the garage, since the only location to place it was facing the street. The home features a limestone entryway, high-pitched gable roofs, dormers and a carriage room over the garage. Designed to fit in between older 1920s Tudor homes, the design emphasis was on creating a contextual blend.

It can be a challenge to build in an older, upscale neighborhood. Not only does a new home need to be created in a similar style to fit in with the rest of the community, but it also needs to be designed to fit well on what is often a small lot. Some of these properties range from 40 to 60 ft. wide.

First, the team does research to know how the homes in the neighborhood originated, how they developed, and what the current lifestyle of their residents is. After a style is decided upon, the next question is how to build the home on a narrow lot. The challenges include maintaining the owners' privacy and not overpowering the neighboring structures. The resulting floor plans, right, reveal what the firm did within tight parameters.

19

20

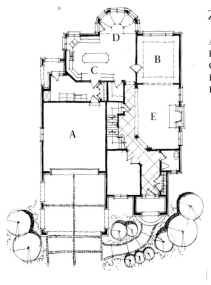

MAIN LEVEL

UPPER LEVEL

ZALESIN FLOOR PLANS

A: Garage
B: Dining Room
C: Kitchen
D: Nook
E: Living Room
F: Master Suite
G: Bedroom 2
H: Bedroom 3
I: Bedroom 4

21

Russell Residence
Rochester Hills, Michigan
1996

The home is an example of formal French design, with emphasis on a variety of window sizes and shapes, and stonework. The entryway is grand, with a 9 ft. door flanked by 12 ft. solid stone columns. Surrounded by hand-split limestone, this majestic exterior design is one of several created by Dominick's firm throughout the private community.

Specially designed for the site, this home is highlighted by a three-story rear turret and a covered terrace that mingles the inside with the elements. Another aspect of Dominick's philosophy is to bring the outdoors in, marrying the exterior with the interior—a method of continuing the flow of style throughout the home. In the summertime, this design of the exterior rear porch enables the homeowner to use both spaces simultaneously.

22

23

D'Agostini Residence
Oakland Township, Michigan
1997

The D'Agostini residence is what the firm calls "French Eclectic," with a symmetry in front, repetitive windows, limestone trim and arched details. The repetitiveness of the windows and the arches above them are typical of this style.

The D'Agostini home is a French Country Manor, with a front turret, fond du lac stone at the entry and drive-under garage arch. A mixture of stone is at the base, as it mimics many of the older homes. This home was designed with high-pitched roof lines, asymmetrical elevation, and balance and form. Size was crucial, especially as it related to how the home fit on the two-acre parcel. A large front yard and open vistas to a pond in the rear yard balance the placement.

25

26

Yellen Residence
Bloomfield Hills, Michigan
2000

This waterfront home was designed with a large, covered porch that wraps around the front. Classified as a "CountryColonial Style," the home featured stone, lapboard and shake siding on the exterior, combined with large, Doric columns around the entryway. The home was designed to blend with the architectural context of the older neighborhood. The exterior was intended to minimize the floor plan size on three levels, totaling up to 11,000 square feet.

27

28

Private Residence
Roscommon, Michigan
1999

This residence was designed to incorporate the ambience of a northern Michigan getaway. The front features a large turret which enables the owners to enjoy multiple views of the golf course, woods, and water. The objective was to create a casual, yet elegant, setting for weekend retreats through the use of natural materials, such as river rock stone and stucco.

29

Schmerin Residence
Franklin, Michigan
1997

In this residence, a Nantucket shingle home incorporates heavy use of limestone and the expected cedar shake siding. But here, the firm starts to introduce the covered porch, cottage windows and exterior trim wood work. The home was developed with an angled garage to balance the house on the site. The stone was hand-selected with a mixture of color tones to blend with the cedar shake siding. The unique design works well on this in-fill neighborhood lot.

30

31

Stollman Residence
Birmingham, Michigan
1999

The challenge for the design of this home was the tight, 50 ft., urban in-fill lot. The size of the lot suited a French Carriage House style, with two garages forming a front axis and French balconies above that overlook a park across the street. The exterior combines stone and stucco, and the interior has unique features, including a stepped-up library and an oval, swooping stairway in the foyer as a center focal point. This home's design was determined partially by the city requirements, while keeping the client's wants and needs in mind. The carriage house look is unique within the street context, yet blends well with surrounding homes.

32. *Original concept elevation sketch.*

33. *French carriage house design on a narrow lot.*

Nida Residence
Rochester Hills, Michigan
1997

In this residence Dominick began to incorporate dormers and a unique roofline in this French Manor style. The exterior features stucco and limestone as two elements that highlight the front facade. The courtyard entry garage was designed to create a European motor court with a colonnade on stone pedestals. The mixture of wood shutters, gas lanterns and unique door hardware put the finishing touches on the project.

34

35

34

C. Menuck Residence
Birmingham, Michigan
2001

This house was designed for an in-fill lot in what is called "Little San Francisco" in Birmingham, Michigan. The Formal French style has a stucco finish, limestone blocks as a foundation and a slate roof. Finishing touches on the exterior include a mahogany hand-carved front door and unique, hand-crafted dormers and window detail.

The interior emphasizes an open floor plan, including a large foyer with a large circular stairway. The kitchen, nook and family room all flow into the family arcade room.

Special attention was given to two large oak trees on the 42 ft. lot. The owners loved the trees, so the firm designed around them, arranging the placement of the entry way and walkway so that the trees would be in perfect alignment with the house. In fact, the linear design of the home is based on its relationship to the tall oak tree in the front.

37

38

A lifestyle is not a type or a brand, it cannot be categorized; rather
a lifestyle is something that is lived and defined by each of us.
—Dominick Tringali

Essence of Lifestyles

According to architect Harwell Hamilton Harris, a "house does not frame the view: it projects the beholder into it." What separates Dominick's homes from others is the inherent emphasis on how a client lives his life—not on the architect's personal tastes and opinions.

Dominick listens carefully to his clients to learn how they live, and he is careful not to impose his own opinions. A house should reflect its inhabitants' lifestyle, he said, not that of the architect's.

Conversations focus on a homeowner's daily routines. A new residence provides the perfect transition for change, so if an owner wants to alter his routine, Dominick will facilitate that adjustment in the design. "I want to make people's lives easier, more livable and enjoyable," he said. "To do that, I need to know where they eat snacks, what their breakfast routine is, how often they have parties and what kind of gatherings they end up being. I even want to know where and when they pay their bills. All of this—and more—determines how the house forms and where it all begins."

Riggio Residence
Grosse Pointe Shores, Michigan
1996

Based on the way these homeowners live, the house was separated—one end completely informal (the master bedroom suite and library as a veritable retreat)—transposed by a formal foyer and dining room at the other end of the house. They wanted formal and casual, but not immediately juxtaposed. The way the house was designed, they practically live in two worlds—without having to go outside.

Drawing from Traditional European styles, the firm incorporated lake views in the front of the house. All rooms and outdoor living space (by way of a two-story terrace) were designed to face Lake St. Clair, while the garage was set in the rear. Inside, the design team created a very open foyer, serving as the central axis for the design.

The dining and family rooms extend off the foyer and feature high ceilings, heavily detailed moldings, palladian windows, and a tray ceiling in the family room. The kitchen and hearth are joined by an open loft and two stories of stacked windows. A separate staircase leads to second-floor bedrooms.

Texture is important in this design. Dominick mixed limestone flooring with painted wood trim and created a marble foyer at the main entry of the home, which opened up to the formal dining room.

2

3

4

Private Residence
Oakland Township, Michigan
1997

The family of this home come and go all the time. That's why Dominick's firm designed a flowing kitchen and family room, where they could easily float between the most comfortable living spaces. The entire residence was created around the family room. A dining room, parlor, and music room grace the front, while a kitchen, breakfast nook, and hearth border the family room.

This design represented a definitive signature style for the firm. With an ornate French exterior—including oval windows, brickwork and limestone detailing—the entryway is framed by formal landscaping, including a courtyard in front.

Mahogany and other exotic woods introduce an Old World flavor. In this house, the flair is in the details. The architects put their stamp on the design via true divided window mullions, fireplace built-ins, wood moldings and a dramatic master bedroom ceiling. By adding a sitting area off the master bedroom, with a two-way fireplace and wet bar, the firm began to make its mark with the retreat-like master suite.

6

7

8

Cohen Residence
West Bloomfield, Michigan
1996

This homeowner lives the casual life of a car collector, which is reflected in his home's California Contemporary design and two-level, eight-car garage. Since the lot slopes, the firm created the house so the owner could access his collectibles—and drive out with the one he needed to use on a daily basis.

The casual style continues inside with eclectic furniture filling the great room—there is no family room. The home has a large kitchen and nook combined with a computer area; the area is inviting, thanks to granite countertops, terracotta floors, butternut cabinets and wood details.

The home sits at the end of a cul-de-sac, bordering wetlands which constrained the design process. As a result, the home hugs the perimeter of the wetlands, which shaped the structure at odd angles (almost an L-shape), so as to meet city requirements.

12. *The great room, centerpoint of the design.*

13.-14. *The lower level, designed in a fun 1950s style.*

15. *Four-car, lower level garage and workshop.*

16. *Kitchen with terra cotta floor and wood cabinets.*

Cohen Residence
Continued

12

13

14

15

Tamaroff Residence

West Bloomfield, Michigan
1998

Although the exterior is Transitional, eclectic touches and clean lines inside create true minimalist décor. In this home, the architecture is the artwork, as evidenced in a hallway created as a gallery, where thick arches, ceiling details and carefully balanced symmetry become awe-inspiring enough to leave the paintings behind. Rounded light coves follow the symmetry of the spaces, as do drop ceilings and barrel vaults.

Because the home backs to a nature preserve, the firm made extensive use of windows, framing the beauty of the woods from virtually all rooms. Fitting in with the owners' casual lifestyle, and marrying the exterior with the interior, a two-way fireplace made of river rock stone became the center point for the kitchen, hearth, and two-story breakfast area.

A Prairie-style kitchen, with exotic woods, granite countertops and a slate backsplash, maintains the outdoorsy feel. The owners specifically wanted no formal rooms. They also wanted separate space for their teenagers while still engendering closeness in the design. This was accomplished by way of a computer loft and sitting area outside the kids' second-floor bedrooms. The parents can retreat to their first-floor suite but gather everyone near the hearth room fireplace for family get-togethers.

17

18

19

20

48

Zalesin Residence
Birmingham, Michigan
1996

From the beginning, this design was a challenge, due to the constraints of a narrow, urban lot and the lifestyle of the young, professional couple who inhabited it. At the time of the design, the Zalesins had no children, but they were trying to plan for the future, said Dominick. They came to him with separate ideas of home, and he combined them to create multi-purpose spaces that could turn from a dining room to a closed-off playroom when they needed it. The key was to fashion flexible spaces that could change with their lifestyle. As a result, the floor plan is open and airy, with no hallways connecting rooms to conserve space. The wall space is limited, and the house goes deep to maximize the lot without bumping up against neighbors.

Dominick created as many private spaces as possible. The second floor is home to a quiet master suite, and a separate bedroom over the garage. The owners also used existing backyard space to create a walled European courtyard.

22

23

Creasy Residence

Birmingham, Michigan
1998

A small house on a large lot, this design was based on the land around it. A front porch wraps around in true Victorian style, looking out to a public park. However, the homeowner has privacy from the public, with the house sitting back on the site to give ample yardage between the park and the home.

The gabled roof reflects a Victorian Cottage style, with an arcade and detailed archways on the exterior which mask the front-entry garage. The details continue inside, with a stairway as a focal point separating space in lieu of walls; which makes it easy for the owner to entertain, a key factor in this person's home life.

The archway into the office/library reinforces the traditional flavor of the house. Oval windows and various details are carried throughout the design.

26

27

25

28

Wayne Residence
Clarkston, Michigan
2000

A Traditional Country Manor home, this creation marked a definitive style of the firm. Combining brick and limestone on the exterior, this house showcases the accumulation of experience of several of the firm's creations, mastering a set style.

"The owners had seen several of our houses before and envisioned themselves living in one of our designs," Dominick said. The brick arcade in front dramatizes the approach up a high hill, and the garage is angled to provide rear entry.

By this point, heavy use of limestone and brick detail throughout the house is a signature move. "Each home we design is unique to each of its homeowners, but the timelessness of brick and stone is obvious in all our projects," said Dominick.

The interior centers around a main axis with an oval stair and warm woods and materials throughout.

29

30

Caponigro Residence
Troy, Michigan
1995

This owner liked to entertain, so his house had to have the ability to support large, comfortable gatherings. The living and dining rooms open up to one large space, as do the kitchen, breakfast nook, and family room. The entire lower level—incorporating a wine room and bar—was designed solely for the purpose of entertaining. Private spaces included a luxurious second floor master suite.

This Traditional Manor house, with limestone and brickwork on the exterior, mixes a formal floor plan with the challenges of a wide but shallow, two-acre parcel. The garage is at an angle, so the home spreads from the front entryway outward. In a way, it makes a statement while melding with the infill of an older neighborhood.

32

33

Life is rich; always changing, always challenging, and we architects have the task of transmitting into wood, concrete, glass and steel, of transforming human aspirations into habitable and meaningful space.
— Arthur Erickson

Harmony Between
Exteriors and Interiors

Architecture by itself does nothing but create fantasies for space. Combine it with a respect for the land on which a structure sits and careful interior designing and you have something that sings, something that borrows the best from the natural elements of the property.

A guiding principle of Dominick's designs is the union of exteriors and interiors, elevating a simple architectural design to a harmonious reflection of the world in which it is found. As Dominick's career developed, he began to concentrate on floor plans as an extension of the "art outside the house—how it blended with the landscape." He stopped leaving décor details to interior designers and began to see those details as part of a bigger picture that is design. For some residences, Dominick designs everything—but even when he doesn't, he presents clients with a complete package. This includes hand-picking designers, landscape artists, and builders who understand his signature style and flair. The final result is the creation of a continuing dialogue between the natural world and the man-made structures that fill it.

"You really have to believe, from day one, that a house is going to flow inside and out," said Dominick. "The two environments become one. When you walk inside, you should feel that same sense that you've captured from the road."

"Alexis" Model
Somerset Showhouse
Kingsridge Subdivision,
Oakland Township, Michigan
2001

Interiors: Dominick Tringali

The ability to design a complete work of art, from start to finish, basement to balusters, paint and portico together, is a rare opportunity in the world of architecture. It's also something that Dominick Tringali relishes. Of course, he only has time for two or three complete designs per year, from architectural scope to décor, and he hand-picks them with care.

This Somerset showhouse was designed in 2001 to model what is possible in a new, upscale, suburban Detroit neighborhood. It was a chance for Dominick's team to put every creative instinct into the throes of design. It is also the best example, they feel, of their finest work to date.

The elevation is a true Italianate style. The floor plan flows, and specialty details tie it all together. A project like this reflects the idea that creating living spaces is about coming up with a livable concept—an ideology that fosters the type of lifestyle the owners are looking for.

Of course, there was no client driving the design, but the ideas and schemes had to appeal to anyone who would walk through the front door.

Backing to a pond, the exterior of this home, as with each house in the Kingsridge Subdivision, emphasizes a lifestyle with entryways and small bodies of water.

2

3

4

"Alexis" Model, Somerset Showhouse
Continued

The entryway continues the Italianate characteristics in a brick paver courtyard leading up to knotty alder wood doors (*Picture 2*). The limestone foyer has a barrel-vault ceiling with light cove that serves as a transition spot between the foyer and the great room. Likewise, the wrought-iron stairway railing has a European essence to it, and was designed as art itself (*Picture 1*).

A music room features faux-painted walls and a textured ceiling with cross beams. Here, Dominick used tapestries to achieve warm walls, reminiscent of European castles. The entire first floor (except the foyer) has clear-stained walnut floors.

The dining room faces the music room and features a built-in cove, dually flanked by sconces to lend a sense of classic formality without dissolving the casual air that dining rooms carry today. The great room has unique windows—rounds above French doorwalls with only horizontal bars on the doors in typical European design.

The same materials crop up again in different uses throughout the house—the limestone powder room reveals a wrought-iron sink, faucet and sconces, modern lighting, and a half-round window above the gilt, gold mirror. The library has a walnut finish with a textured ceiling and cross-beams. Here, architecture accessorizes via built-ins; the room opens out to a covered porch (*Picture 4*).

6

7

8

60

"Alexis" Model, Somerset Showhouse
Continued

The open kitchen, like so many kitchens today, features a stove with an old stone look, a fireplace, pine cabinets, and generous seating at a long and narrow farm table. Hanging pot racks and wrought-iron fixtures accentuate the fluidity of the interior, as do the mixture of textures—slate backsplash, green island, granite countertops (*Picture 7*).

Upstairs, the master bedroom has a private, screened-in porch and sitting area with a three-sided fireplace. The master bedroom ceiling is backlit with a lay-in wrought-iron design painted metallic to add ambience and offset the lighter walls. The marble master bath has intricate border trim and mosaic details, in addition to two mosaic niches framing the tub and four Roman columns. As is evident in today's popularity of large, cozy master suites and smaller dining rooms, this showhouse appropriately portrayed the lifestyle of a person who wants to come home to a relaxing retreat, leaving the chaos of the work world outside. In his creations, Dominick wants to show that people no longer have to leave their homes to find serenity.

The three additional bedrooms include two children's rooms and a guest bedroom. The walls in the girl's room are awash with lavender paint and accented by sparkly butterflies. The boy's room is done in a jungle theme with knotty pine walls. A bamboo wallpapered ceiling, creative moldings and hand-painted doorknobs complete the picture. In the guest bedroom, a travel theme was created using old framed photographs as art and stacked suitcases as a table. A telescope and a 10 ft. ceiling maximize the drama of a canopy bed.

10

11

12

13. *Lower level recreation room and arcade.*

14. *Colorful boxing ring for cardio training and kickboxing workouts.*

15. *Billiards room adjacent to English pub and wine room.*

"Alexis" Model, Somerset Showhouse
Continued

Typical of many of Dominick's plans, this house also features a large lower level—3,000 sq. ft.—where the fictitious owners could retreat for relaxation and entertainment. A game room and arcade area border a wood-paneled media room with theater seating for 12. Instead of an exercise room, the design team picked up on current workout trends and created a colorful boxing ring for cardio training and kickboxing. The level finishes off with an old English pub, billiards, wine room and humidor. These rooms utilize earthy materials—slate for the floor and stone and clay for the tiles.

Done as a charity effort, this showhouse is a joint effort on the part of Dominick Tringali Architects, the Somerset Collection, and Moceri Development. The event raised more than $150,000 for local charities, and was held at Kingsridge Subdivision in the Oaklands Project, Oakland Township.

13

14

Schechter Residence
Franklin, Michigan
1997

An acre-and-a-half swath of melodious landscape set the scene for this posh, wooded retreat that was easy to call home. There was no choice but to design this home into the woods, for tall trees were everywhere.

This design came out of a natural respect for the order of things, the backyard falling off into the meadows until you could not discern where one ended and the other began.

"The homeowner and I wanted to capture the essence of a country manor," said Dominick, "so we created a carriage house feeling with stable doors at the entry, and we designed a garage that looks more like something you'd find on a farm a century ago."

A key to marrying interiors and exteriors is using the same materials inside and out, according to Dominick. Castle rock from New York (long used to build foundations in older houses) is featured on the exterior and also in the stone fireplace and back hall flooring (*Pictures 21 & 23*).

17

18

16

19

Schechter Residence
Continued

It was expressly important for the texture and materials to convey the sense that the house had been there for decades, perhaps longer. The single professional who would live there wanted a Western-style interior made almost entirely of natural materials—leathers, knotty alder wood and pine. A mantle from an old barn and wood beams and ceilings capture the outdoor feel, once again providing a critical tie from exterior to interior.

The country kitchen has a wood-burning stove and pizza oven—the materials here are modern, but the feel stays Old World, thanks to a cutting-edge Viking oven set into the crook where you'd expect to find an old-fashioned heating element. Additionally, high glass, transoms, and faux painting continue the aura.

The dining room has a butler's pantry and exposed wine rack. The powder room and light fixtures feature a classic, almost retro design in the wall sconces and pedestal sink.

Yet in the deep recesses of the home, some spaces will fool you—in an arbitrary, somewhat bold way, the carriage-house over the garage is nothing like the frontier essence of the rest of the house. Rather, it is an ultra-modern exercise and fitness center, with a sauna, juice bar and open ceilings.

20

DETAIL $\frac{FF}{4}$

21

22

23. *Living room/dining room view*
24. *Kitchen/nook.*
25. *Alcove to master suite.*

Private Residence
Towncenter Towers
Southfield, Michigan
1997

For this project, the client requested that Dominick combine six 1,000 sq. ft. apartments into one modern 6,000 sq. ft. condo. The biggest challenge lay in the inner workings of the existing plumbing, mechanical and lighting systems, which couldn't be transfixed, despite the entire gutting and remodeling of what is nearly two-thirds of the floor.

Because ceiling heights were fixed, Dominick designed drops to create the aura that the homeowner sought. Although this space is located in the middle of a complex, commercial development in suburbia, this home is reminiscent of a spacious, upscale apartment off New York's Central Park.

The modern spin begins with alcove and ceiling details and continues in the surrounding light coves. Curved, glass walls give a loft feel. The design revolves largely around the owners' extensive art collection,

23

24

FLOOR PLAN

Private Residence
Continued

resulting in open, flowing spaces and wall lengths designed to meld with the art as if in a gallery. Likewise, lighting schemes were designed around accentuating the paintings.

The firm planned the lighting and ceiling details and worked closely with the interior designer on some of the finishes. Dominick's staff was involved in choosing wall surfaces, sconces, and track lighting, which aided in designing specialty niches throughout the home to highlight the artwork.

The design borrows characteristics from the owners, a Renaissance type, worldly couple with a second home in Florida and high-profile advertising and TV careers. Adjectives like "slick," "high-profile," and "cutting-edge" are easy to find in the design.

"We build relationships with our clients," explained Dominick. "We ride the journey together, and the resulting design is a reflection of the time we spend together, talking, relating, identifying distinct elements of the way they want to live."

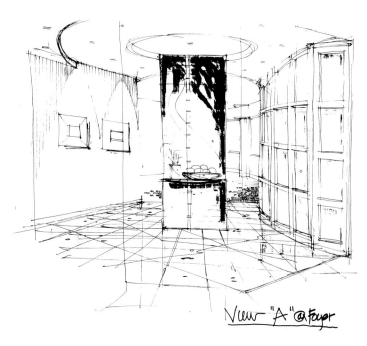

Private Residence in Poppleton Park

Birmingham, Michigan
2000
Interiors by: Dominick Tringali

While so many of Dominick's clientele want something new, cutting-edge and full of possibility, they also want their residence to feel like it's been there for 100 years. This English Tudor design required research to appropriately create something that reflects the charm of yesteryear while incorporating the conveniences of today. From the landscaping to the interior details, everything came together in a reflection of that style. Each room was created independently to flow with the rest of the design.

A screened-in porch features cedar beams imported from England. Inside, the design mimics details from English mansions, including Meadowbrook Hall, Rochester, Michigan. The details include the library and interior arcades, which use stone instead of wood elements.

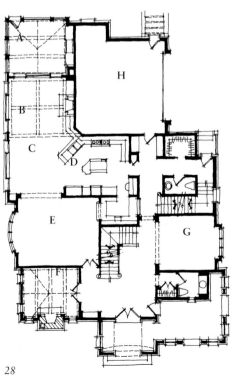

FIRST FLOOR PLAN

A: Screened Porch
B: Hearth
C: Nook
D: Kitchen
E: Family Room
F: Library
G: Dining Room
H: Two-Car Garage

28. *(on previous page) First floor layout.*

29. *(on previous page) Overall view of residence from the street.*

30. *Concept sketch for entry.*

31. *Specially designed front door, hand carved.*

32. *Alcove to powder room with barrel vault ceiling.*

33. *Post and beam screened-in porch.*

Private Residence in Poppleton Park
Continued

Today's trends favor open floor plans. This home has no formal living room but compensates with a large, formal dining room reminiscent of British castles.

The lower level has window wells and stone detail accompanying a steam shower and locker room under the garage. The 1,500 sq. ft. gym features a 12 ft. ceiling.

The exterior was dictated entirely by the lot. Adjacent to a park, the team oriented the views to maximize the natural setting and incorporate full use of the sunrise and sunset. Privacy was of maximum importance, so plantings and pine trees were brought in, creating an outdoor living space with a freestanding fireplace.

30

31

32

Water is the one substance from which the earth can conceal nothing.
— Jean Giraudoux, *The Madwoman of Chaillot* (1945)

1

Waterfront Homes

Dominick Tringali Architects designs in Midwestern states that have thousands of lakes. It faces the unique challenges of designing for waterfront views while protecting homes from the harsh elements that lake and river properties can present.

Additionally, the cost of such properties has risen so dramatically that affordable parcels are usually narrow—and thus harder to work with. Facing the usual restrictions of waterfront drop-off, sloping terrain, and view-oriented architecture, the firm also has to create plans that avoid blocking a neighbor's views and that maintain the character of the lake.

In general, waterfront homes are casual, deemed so by the laid-back, outdoorsy lifestyle of the people who live in them. Waterfront residents often forego formal rooms to make it easier to move throughout the house. The most important element of these designs is capturing stunning views from as many rooms as possible, which means incorporating a dramatic use of glass and very tall windows whenever possible. Dominick's firm designs about 20 waterfront homes per year.

Brandon Residence

Grand Rapids, Michigan
On the Thorn Apple River
1997

Featuring stone, shake, and horizontal lap siding in a shingle style, this home incorporates columns and heavy bracket work with an overall cottage feel. Only two rooms—the dining room and the library—do not have a river view. The rest have unobstructed views of the water, achieved by orienting everything on angles to critically place each room.

As well, the firm had to seal off the side of the house that bordered on public access to the waterfront. Thus, they maximized the views on the other side of the house, and placed the garage with few windows on the public side so the owners wouldn't be staring at strangers and boat launches.

"This style is very vernacular, yet very ornate," said Dominick. To carry that theme through on the inside, he and his staff introduced painted finishes, niches, and Prairie-style window designs. The great room has a barrel-vault ceiling with light cove. Upper balconies create loft spaces.

2

3. *Exterior screened porch detail.*

4. *Great room with view of river.*

5. *Floor plans of first and second levels.*

6. *Front courtyard entry.*

Brandon Residence
Continued

3

4

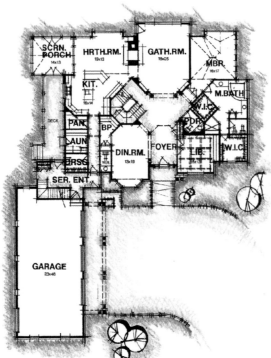

FIRST FLOOR PLAN

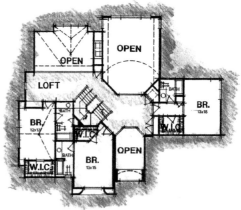

SECOND FLOOR PLAN

5

7. *Elevation, as viewed from the center of the lake.*
8. *Kitchen/hearth and nook, all with views to the water.*
9. *Great room vista as you enter the foyer.*

Price Residence
Orchard Lake, Michigan
On Upper Straits Lake
1996

This was an extremely difficult site to reach, due to its long and narrow layout and a 30 ft. drop from the house platform to the edge of the lake. Both the architect and the landscape architect collaborated to devise retaining walls which could be integrated into the design, and created a backyard first, before the house was constructed. Clearly, landscaping was integral from day one.

As with any waterfront house, Dominick and the owners wanted to maximize the number of views. All spaces, except the library and the dining room, face the waterfront, with large windows opening reflections onto the lake.

The kitchen nook and hearth open to each other, and a greenhouse overlooks the kitchen from an open loft above. The greenhouse was intended to provide more light because of its high placement above cabinets while adequately blocking the view of a nearby neighbor.

Large boulders, found along the lakeshore, create a terraced effect with a ramping walkway down to the lake. The interior has strong embellishments, with lighting as a main focus.

"The key to this design is that the clients wanted to keep the house livable. The lower level is totally for entertainment and lake access. In most waterfront houses, we create 'a lake room' that provides direct access from the water, keeping sand, dust, and dirt out of the other living spaces," Dominick said.

7

8

9

Moceri Residence

Glen Arbor, Michigan
On Lake Michigan
1995

Since the owners frequent this home in the warmer months, it had to be a place to get away, in traditional Northern Michigan style, while still incorporating their love of contemporary flair. Traditional Victorian shingling and styling blends the home with the neighborhood.

This structure grew out of the shoreline. River rock comprises the base and is brought inside via a massive, two-story fireplace, the focal point between the great room, kitchen and nook. Soaring windows expose an enchanting view of the lake. Antler fixtures and natural woods mix with modern conveniences for the interior style.

The covered terrace is crucial for bad weather days and rain. An extended balcony combines with lower level recreational space to entertain guests staying in the home's five bedrooms.

Situated on the roaring waters of one of the Great Lakes (winter ice dams build as high as 13 ft.), Dominick's staff made sure this house had enough glass to maximize the view, but they also ensured it was stable enough to weather the elements.

10

11

13. *Original design sketch of rear porch.*

14. *View of foyer with T-stair and unique chandelier.*

15. *Kitchen eating area.*

16. *View of great room with barrel ceiling and stone fireplace.*

Moceri Residence
Continued

13

14

15

Private Residence
Sylvan Lake, Michigan
On Sylvan Lake
1999

The homeowner wanted to mimic a true cottage style, so piers taper into lap siding with outdoor balconies and clear bottom windows for a pristine lake view. The lot is narrow, so the garage was carved into the lower level, shaving off a dramatic, 20 ft. slope in the rear.

Harkening back to the style of the owner's grandmother's cottage, the interior features white, painted trim, white cabinets, and other details inspired by 1920s Bungalows. That style is reflected again in railings, inside and out. Roof lines bury much of the second floor rooms in the design, giving the home an overall balance within its site. The cobblestone stonework took five months to install.

The hardest part of this project was considering the close proximity of neighboring homes along with designing for a tapering 45 ft. wide slope. "You have to consider the effect of each house on the ones around it," Dominick said.

18

19

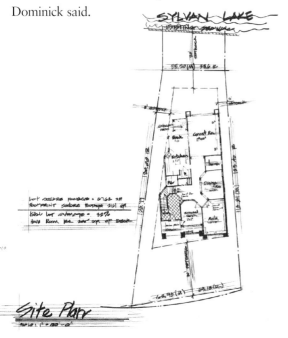

17

Strickstein Residence
Orchard Lake, Michigan
on Orchard Lake
2000

Low-lining roofs and stone ledges mix with brick and siding to create a classic contemporary exterior on this lakefront home. The stone carries through to the interior in the form of great room archways, foyer flooring, fireplace and piers that face a covered terrace.

In true lake style, this home has no formal rooms, but the great room features a massive, three-way stone fireplace that opens to the kitchen and nook. Again, large expanses of glass face full vistas of the lake.

This lake lot had its own difficult restrictions—the height requirement and lot coverage standards instituted by the city allowed for only so much house to be constructed on a percentage of the lot. As well, there were sight-line setbacks from adjoining neighbors.

"We ended up with a walkout ranch design with first-level living spaces. Natural materials inside and out carry through a stylistic flow, mirrored in terraces on both levels," Dominick said.

22

21

23

Strickstein Residence
Continued

25

26

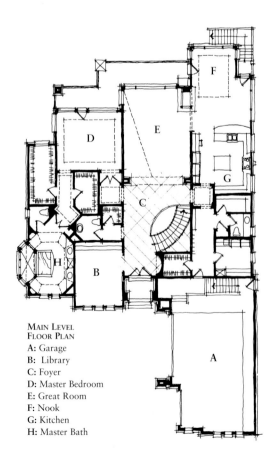

**MAIN LEVEL
FLOOR PLAN**
A: Garage
B: Library
C: Foyer
D: Master Bedroom
E: Great Room
F: Nook
G: Kitchen
H: Master Bath

27

28

Rimar Residence
Lake Angelus, Michigan
On Lake Angelus
2000
Project Designer: Jason Ruthig

The project presented, perhaps, the toughest restrictions yet, including historic parameters, township ordinances, and very specific desires of the owners. For example, the ordinances specified the massing of the house, the height specifications, and proximity to neighbors. The grade could neither be moved nor adjusted.

After tearing down a former structure, Dominick's team used existing terrain around which to build this house. The garage was placed toward the street, and has carriage house space above it. Stucco and stone highlight mahogany beams at the entry and at the lake view side. Large, two-story spaces provide views to the lake.

30

31

Angeli Residence

Birchville, Michigan
On Lake Huron
1999

Designed in New York Transitional style, this
house sits on a large lake parcel with a 30 ft.
cliff dropping off to the waterfront. In the
winter, the drop-off fills with 20 ft. of ice,
so structural stability is crucial.

Owned by young professionals, who are
raising a family of three, the main floor was
designed in such a way that the parents could
be busy with their own tasks while still able
to watch their children play.

The home has a nautical theme, with a
large turret and porthole windows. There
is no first-floor formal area, and the kitchen,
nook, and great room all open to each other.
A three-car carriage house garage and an
additional two-car space connect via a
breezeway.

Government requirements complicated the
placement of the house on the land. The
entire structure sits on an angle, to catch
certain degrees for optimal lake views.
A rear library serves as a sort of observatory
(complete with nautical telescope) to watch
freighters on the lake.

33

34

98

33. *Front entry.*

34. *Original concept sketch.*

35. *Rear elevation from Lake Huron.*

35

We try to put as much art into the architecture as
we can, so the architecture itself becomes part of
the artwork of the home. —Dominick Tringali

Special Rooms, Elements and Details

Room design and layout can influence a home's entire personality, so placement is crucial. Dominick breaks down each house and creates a priority of parts in ascending order of importance for the owners. Each client emphasizes a different space, and each space conveys a different aura. "I'm not the type of architect who would put dramatic ceilings in every room just to do it," he said. "You need to emphasize spaces that need emphasis and downplay other spaces to make critical rooms feel important."

Some people make their impact in the foyer, while others want to send a message with a large, oversized kitchen or family room. You can learn something about a person simply by walking through his front door, and Dominick capitalizes on those values.

His staff of designers considers special details and room placement critical in the design process. They are arranged at certain axis points and views where they have the most impact. "I like a lot of niches and artwork details," said Dominick. That's why, sometimes, we'll do a swooping dramatic stair or a unique stepped ceiling detail. Anything to emphasize a client's taste."

2. This free-standing, traditional stairway is integrated with the rest of the house. Placed against a window for a see-through effect, the full view of the stairway encapsulates a sense of interaction with the rest of the home.

3. This example of a contemporary foyer highlights the artistic value of the stairway as sculpture. Stainless steel tube piping enwraps a drywall stairwell.

4. A unique raised panel detail is incorporated into the stair and archway.

5. This rotunda foyer features a semi-circular, winding stairway and detailed ceiling. It is set off to the side of the house, with a large chandelier accentuated by a stepped ceiling.

6. This traditional stairway was made from mahogany with wainscoting at the ends and wood balusters along the sides. A segregated marble foyer accents the dual stairway, heavy woodworking and detailing of this European Traditional residence.

Foyers and Stairways

The foyer began as a public gathering space of a theater, auditorium, or other civic building. It was a place where people could meet, promenade, mingle, and walk. It served as the gateway that bridged the harsh realities of the exterior with the warm activity of what was going on inside, a transition between the public and the performers.

When foyers began to be translated into residential spaces, they served as the focal point of a home. Originating from the traditional vestibule, their purpose was to provide a small space where visitors could remove coats and shoes and leave the cold outside. In fact, to that end, they used to have a set of double doors—one facing the outside and another leading into the home—to isolate the elements. Eventually, as people gained affluence, they started to use the foyer as a reception hall, much like in the castles of Europe. Nowadays, dramatic entries are giving way to less defined, more interactive spaces that start off the flow of a house, overlapping into usable spaces.

2

3

4

5

Kitchens

For centuries, the kitchen has reflected the way people want to live. From Neanderthal days, when early man first learned to put a stone on the fire, until the 19th century, when the kitchen and dining room were still segregated, lines were drawn between sustaining life and living it.

Today, the kitchen is the most popular room in the house—it's where Americans spend half of their at-home time, according to John Driemen, author of *Kitchens: Exciting Ideas for Creating the Kitchen You've Always Wanted*. In fact, remodeling this all-important room is the most popular large-scale home fix-up project, Driemen said, with roughly $17.8 billion spent annually in this direction.

According to author Terrence Conran, in his *Kitchen Book*, "A kitchen provides physical and spiritual nourishment, and for many homes is now the heart and soul of family life."

In Dominick Tringali's designs, the kitchen has become the most eagerly anticipated focal point of a home. Even for individuals who don't cook much, it has become a meeting place where people congregate, friends gather, and daily lives happen.

7. *A large table enhances this kitchen's sense of country. Most of Dominick's kitchens have high ceilings, which add volume and space. Likewise, many have wood floors, lending an organic warmth to the room. That happened here, where the maple floor and cabinets made the room cohesive. "What everyone likes about the country kitchen is its roominess and space, bringing us back to Grandma's house, that old farm feeling that people always liked."*

8. *Here, the design aims to create a warm kitchen, open to an adjacent octagonal nook. The heart of an English Tudor home, it features painted trim, arched windows, a slate floor, granite countertops, and cherry wood accents.*

9-10. *Key elements in this country kitchen include a pizza oven and fireplace that connect to the warm wood cabinetry. Modern appliances blend well into the Old World aspects of the kitchen, and a hanging pot rack serves as an integral bridge between the two.*

11. *Reflecting the company's versatility of design, this modern kitchen makes extensive use of light by way of high windows, a corner outlook over the sink, and peaked skylights above the island. This design emphasizes the functional, with clean lines that blend the contemporary exterior with the functional interior. A wood floor and granite counters integrate the natural area outside the house with the stark highlight of stainless steel appliances.*

7

8

9

10

12. *Light floods into this room, stressing the ceiling, volume and windows. The adjacent serene sitting area faces the back of the house.*

13. *Another traditional bedroom, this design has a small tray ceiling, a built-in fireplace and niches. The two-way fireplace is adjacent to a sitting room that ties the spaces together.*

14. *Here, the child-like décor, style of window, and wall and window placement dictate in the architectural design phase where the bed and dresser would go.*

15. *This children's room is playful, despite architecturally sophisticated details like the high ceiling and round-top windows. Décor played a key role in translating the space into a fun place to be.*

16. *This is a traditional bedroom, with a fireplace, viewing windows to the backyard, and a high ceiling with molding that wraps around the full length of the room.*

Bedrooms

In post World War II American homes, the bedrooms are placed upstairs and the daytime living spaces downstairs, separating the functions of the home. Today, parents aren't as concerned about being on the same floor as their children—in fact, the master bedroom has become a home of its own, with sitting rooms, majestic bathrooms, and sometimes exercise or computer areas providing privacy and entertainment away from the rest of the house.

Dominick Tringali uses the master bedroom suite as a retreat for busy homeowners. Incorporating fireplaces, lounges and work spaces, the bedroom is no longer a place to just go in the evening. People are spending more of their home time there, reading and contemplating. This trend rejects the fast pace of today's society, from which people want an easy escape.

12

13

14

15

17. *This media room, designed and detailed by Dominick, features cherry wood and stepped theater seating for 12 to 16 people. The predesign accounted for acoustics and surround sound.*

18. *Billiards rooms are no longer separate from the rest of the recreational space. Here, media and game time flow together for maximum interaction.*

19. *A bar/kitchenette area is crucial for overall enjoyment, so homeowners don't have to traipse up and down the stairs to supplement down-time activities with snacks. Usually, the refreshment space is designed as the center point, drawing together all other recreational spaces.*

20.-21. *These wine rooms incorporate natural materials, including a slate floor, clay, and tiles to hold wine bottles. A humidor is incorporated into the rear. Natural, cold, hard materials maintained a cool temperature for wine and convey a true cellar feeling and appearance, inspired by vineyard dwellings.*

Wine Room/Media Room

During the past two decades, high-end homes have been incorporating wine cellars and media rooms in the lower level. Rather than going out after a hard day's work, people want to bring entertainment home, Dominick said. Wine cellars and humidors are the boldest example of upscale enjoyment, and media rooms pair movie facilities with places to play advanced video games. The whole family can enjoy these rooms simultaneously.

17

18

19

20

22. *This exercise space is adjacent to the master suite. Built over the garage, it connects easily to the master bathroom and is flooded with light.*

23-24. *Home gyms now incorporate dry saunas, steam showers, lockers and hot tubs with a fireplace. All help to bring the fresh outdoor feeling inside.*

25. *This basketball court is designed in a two-story, double basement space.*

26. *As part of its clean, contemporary style, this exercise room uses glass block in a minimalist design. It is surrounded by windows for an open-air feeling.*

Exercise Rooms

Just like entertainment spaces, workout spaces provide homeowners the opportunity to exercise at all hours without the inconvenience of having to travel to a gym. Design and room placement, though, depend on the residents' lifestyle. If it's a morning routine, they may want an exercise space adjacent to the bedroom and bathroom, for ease of showering and getting ready for work. Although styles can vary, most exercise rooms emphasize clean lines and a contemporary design. Windows can make them open and airy, but some people prefer darker, more industrial-looking spaces reminiscent of traditional gyms.

22

23

24

25

27. *Architectural detail is utilized in the wall sconces, stone around the arch, and on the walls of this powder room, for old-world romance.*

28. *The ladder conveys intellectuality in the design of this open and airy library. A bay window and built-ins are details that must be decided upon at the beginning of the process.*

29. *A barrel-vaulted ceiling, light coves, and an end niche, all lead this hallway dramatically to the master bathroom. Here, trim work and detail achieve a sense of presence and serenity on the way to the bathtub.*

30. *This parlor entry is emphasized with wood trim and a thicker archway, which was predesigned in the initial concepts.*

31. *The library can be an apt place for detail, especially dramatic beam ceilings, woodworking, and built-ins.*

Miscellaneous Details

The truth is in the details. These pages show the tiny touches that mark the company's unique style and thought process throughout each home.

27

28

29

30

32. With a round window high above the mirror, this bathroom has natural light without sacrificing privacy. A two-way, free-floating fireplace is the focal point between rooms.

33. Detail and placement of the tub and vanities are critical in the design of each bath.

34. This master bathroom, contemporary in flavor, has a high ceiling and plant shelves that shine light up to emphasize height. Granite surfaces and carefully placed plants reflect the nature outside the windows.

35. Ceilings can be dramatic—even in a master bathroom like this, which features a barrel-vault ceiling held up by four columns to Romanesquely frame the tub. Ceilings convey drama and volume in the smaller spaces.

Master Baths

The bathroom or powder room of any home is the finishing touch of a home. It is probably the least viewed, but the most used. When Dominick and his associates create a bathroom, they take care to make the room very personalized to its homeowner's lifestyle. How a person feels about himself during the day often starts with the moments spent in this room. Therefore, details such as the amount and angle of light that shines through the room, the type of vanity, and the spaciousness or closeness of the room's elements are arranged to reflect the homeowner, to give him a chance to start the day out right.

"We spend a tremendous amount of time on these rooms because they give back as much as we put into them," said Dominick. "We want them to be special to all who daily inhabit them."

32

33

34

114

The development of a home is a dialogue between both
client and architect to achieve the ultimate goal in fulfilling
their needs and dreams. — Dominick Tringali

A Walk Through the Process

1. *Exterior view of the corporate headquarters.*

2. *Main conference room with custom mahogany built-ins.*

3. *Gallery hallway displaying various photos of the firm's works.*

The firm's headquarters, based in Bloomfield Hills, Michigan, aptly reflects the philosophy and process that the firm employs on every project. In his headquarters, Dominick wants a residential feel, despite the corporate aspect of its use. The hallway is lit by modern, halogen spotlights. The dome in the conference room would be appropriate in someone's dining room, but here it works to convey a sense of being among friends, gathering over a leisurely meal for all to enjoy. The warm woods and stones of the floor and walls, desks and nooks, could be found in a kitchen or home office. The niches for displaying home models are similar to the vistas and viewpoints that Dominick likes to highlight in homes.

Special touches don't cost more—they just take thought, Dominick said. "When people ask, 'What are you all about?' I take them for a tour around our building."

It's quiet as you enter the initial foyer area. The clean lines and rich woods beckon, and then you start to feel the hum of activity, the intellectual generation of talent. Beyond the glass-etched conference room doors and down the spotlit hall, the bustle begins. Architects and designers cross from office to office, brainstorming, thinking, creating.

In true Transitional form, the offices combine light and dark woods, and feature exposed ceilings with modern, clean lines. Some spaces have the look of an urban loft, while corner offices are quiet and subtle with French doors propped open to facilitate flow.

Everything about this office space says new but traditional, style but experimental. It aptly reveals the aggressive, eager nature of the employees who work there. Still, the office pays homage to the traditions of their field, in architectural relief bookends and a Victorian door panel that hangs on display in the conference room. "Architecture is art," said Dominick. "We mix materials and finishes, we create warmth with exotic woods. Everything that my clients experience in our offices are key elements that we try to bring into the homes we create."

Upon leaving the office the first time, the client has many concepts and images to consider. The exchange of ideas yields a vast amount of potential. Dominick said he likes to build houses that are "places where ideas can't help but collide." So as he and a new client enter each new architectural endeavor, he treats it as if it were the first, a clean page, an open field. The entire range of architectural form is laid out ahead of the two of them, and the adventure is about to begin.

2

3

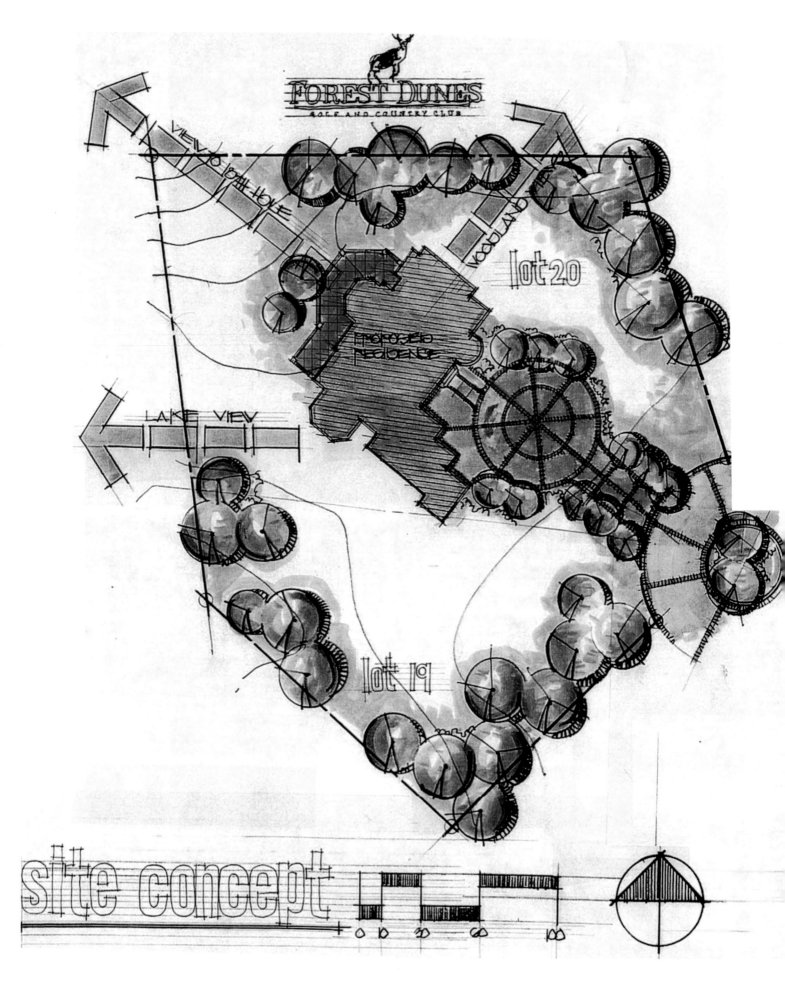

FOREST DUNES
GOLF AND COUNTRY CLUB

VIEW 6th HOLE

WOODLAND

lot 20

PROPOSED RESIDENCE

LAKE VIEW

lot 19

site concept

0 10 30 60 100

Clients could suppose that the symmetry and geometry that they see in Dominick's office—the tall windows without clutter, natural light cascading onto muted fixtures—will be reflected in the home they may ask him to create. They could guess what he might come up with, but they won't be guessing for long. Dominick's emphasis on communication thrusts itself into the beginning of every working relationship, just as he takes out marker and paper to sketch for his clients.

The process of creating a living, breathing design begins with the interpersonal. Dominick invites clients (most of whom come by way of referral) to come in for an initial get-to-know-you, where they sit down together, talk out their dreams, and create a plan of action. Everything depends on an equal give-and-take; creating residential space is about building a workable relationship that, like the home he hopes to build, will stand the test of time.

Dominick approaches a prospective client as a new friend—someone to get to know, someone to impress, someone with whom to relate. He shows a variety of previous work, and they talk, long and hard, about the ideas that are floating in the air around them. At that first meeting, he provides a process overview, explaining every step of the way, and sends clients home with an assignment: to consider and visit as many as 10 current projects that exhibit various styles and characteristics.

The second session is the program meeting, where they begin to get specific. Everyone settles in to talk about the clients' lifestyle and the type of house desired, their needs now and in the future.

In the next step, a site plan is created. The land and the house come together, a coherent package that must flow. Dominick walks the site, looking for major views and setback issues like wetlands or city restrictions. He considers adjacent homes, topography and grade, and then determines where on the property the sun rises and sets. All of these factors tell him where the house should go. (*Picture 4*)

Throughout this phase, the client is provided with two to three small-scale drawings, revealing options for the site. The exchange of feedback continues until all involved can agree on room size, square footage and layout of the overall spaces (*Pictures 6 & 7*).

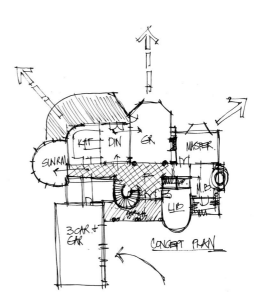

5

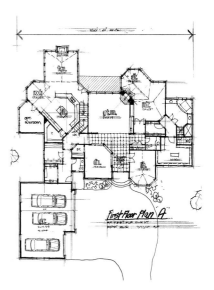

6

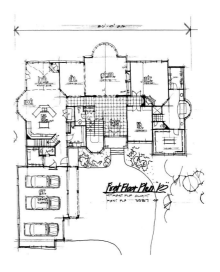

7

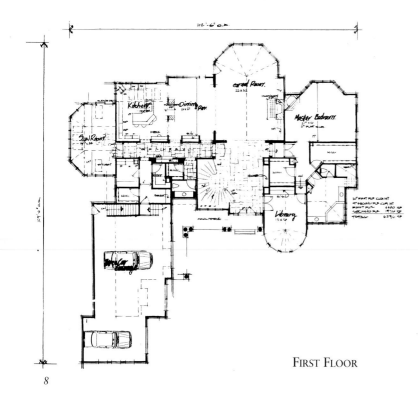

FIRST FLOOR

8

In the schematic design phase, the designers formulate a building program and an overall concept, including spatial relationships. They construct 1/4 inch preliminary drawings and pull in other team members, including builders and interior designers. With an emphasis on teamwork, each party adds detail and intricacies to the plan. At this point, they begin to discuss budget and how to work within cost parameters. Another aspect the team views are the elevations. They also do various block cuts to make sure the end result meets both the clients' and aesthetic needs.

Ninety-eight percent of the homes Dominick Tringali designs are built—a surprisingly high number—in an age when some architects see only half of their designs reaching fruition. The key, he says, is staying in tune with market costs in order to develop houses that meet real budgets. Budget adherence depends largely on the complexity of the initial design, layout and interior finishes.

As the coordinator of the project and design concept, it is Dominick's challenge to make sure all parties involved are working together to meet the clients' goals and aspirations. All details from furniture placement to venting details are reviewed and incorporated into the final construction document.

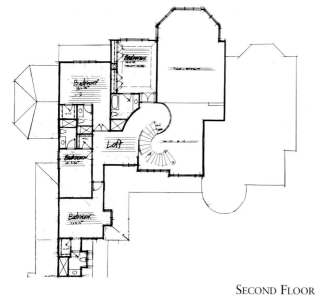

SECOND FLOOR

9

In the final design development phase, the staff combine elevations and final floor plans, making adjustments for proportion and scale. The plans provide clients with a four-sided design, which includes the back of the home and side views, ensuring that the structure looks equally impressive from every angle.

The interior designer involved with this process must provide adequate input about what will work on the inside, while the builder can look at structural aspects and add an appropriate assessment, too. In the end, the firm provides its clients with a complete, workable package that is unique and on budget.

10 CONCEPTUAL ELEVATION

FIRST FLOOR

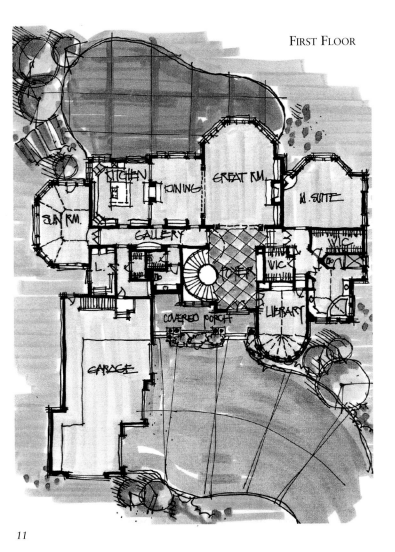

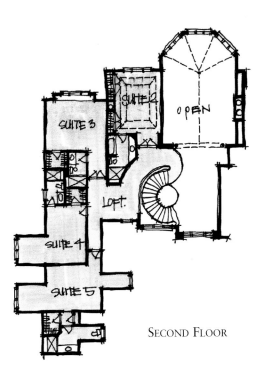

SECOND FLOOR

11

12

13. *Initial entry sketch.*

14. *Construction documents with the details.*

15. *Completed entry design.*

13

Final revisions are based on budget, size, and décor, and then come the construction documents. These are the drawings that a house is built by, and they must be flawless enough to secure permits and the proper approvals necessary. Each set of drawings at this phase gives detailed information for carpenters, bricklayers, roofers, and other key craftsmen who will work together to construct the home. Exterior elevations, window openings, porches, and column and chimney details must be detailed for each trade, in order to achieve the look that Dominick's designs are known for.

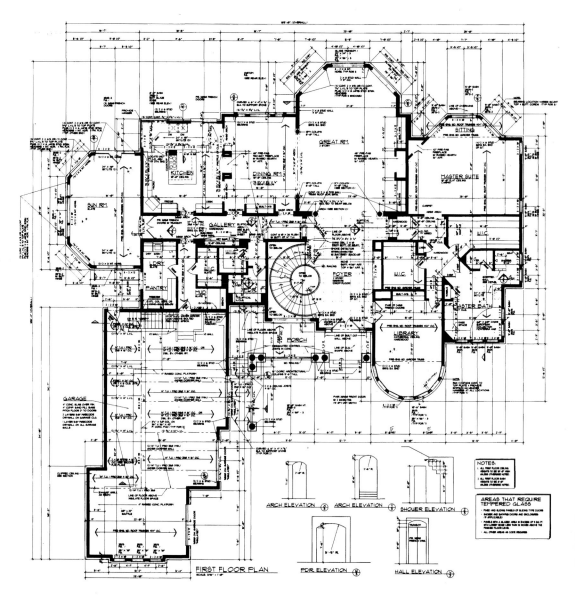

14

Three other areas comprise the final package:

■ The mechanical/HVAC plan integrates the heating and cooling systems with the architectural design. Dominick's firm coordinates the ductwork and furnaces as well as overseeing the insulation, an unusual skill for residential architects.

■ The electrical plan incorporates all the lighting and switching, which creates the ambience and romance of the house. This work should never be left to outside sources who don't know the project, according to Dominick.

■ The architectural interior details and trim, in conjunction with the project's interior designer, specifies openings and archways, doors, built-in bookshelves, stairs and fireplaces. Interior selection is the final step, where the team is involved in selections of tile, wall color and draperies.

Once a set of drawings is completed, permits are obtained. Then the construction begins. Dominick and his team supervise each step of the project, and follow through on all phases to completion.

Near the end of the construction period, final materials for interiors are selected, and the team advises in any way they can. Accordingly, they also work with the landscape architect to put the finishing touches on the surrounding grounds of the new home. Such painstaking attention is paid so that the client can be assured that the same care that went into the planning is being carried through to his complete satisfaction.

16

All of my homes never reach completion;
they are always growing and eventually
blooming into a timeless art piece.
—Dominick Tringali

Current and Future Homes

This chapter is a selection of works that are currently "on the boards" or in the initial construction stages. They represent the latest ideas and trends that Dominick's staff have developed. With each project, the design team sets new goals while attempting to push the envelope with every detail and drawing. As a result, they create new concepts that continue to evolve over time, developing and enhancing a variety of architectural styles.

Each of these residences began as a napkin sketch, evolved into a detailed plan, and is now on its way to becoming a reality in its environment. This evolution is a process each project will experience from start to finish. As such, these projects receive approximately six to eight months of design and development time and 14 to 18 months of construction. Some will be completed in the near future, others not until 2004.

Although their lives have just begun, once completed, these homes will grow and evolve along with the families living within them. As we have seen with other examples of Dominick's work, they will become timeless pieces of architecture for generations to come.

Dutton Road Estate
Oakland Township, Michigan

Project Architect: Randy Hatchard
Project Designer: Jason Ruthig
Builder: Vito Anthony Homes
Interior Designer: D.J. Kennedy

This project is a traditional European design exhibiting over 21,000 sq. ft. of living space. The estate displays two formal points of entry, each supported with a custom motor court, private garage, powder room and walk in closet. Upon entering the home, one will experience dramatic two-story barrel ceilings, highly detailed woodwork and customized glass. The first floor features an oversized kitchen, essential for all types of social gatherings and a first floor master suite for easy accessibility. The second floor features five large bedrooms, each with a private bath and walk-in closet as well as a reading loft which leads to a third story bar and rec area. Lastly, the lower level is highlighted by a custom in-ground pool and full support facility, which include his and her bath, dressing area, sauna and steam. In addition, the lower level also features a home theater, billiards area, sunken golf room and elevator which runs to all four levels. The façade of the home is highly detailed with both brick and stone and contains many covered and uncovered landscaped terraces and porches. Surrounded by 20 acres of natural landscape, the estate is softened with both public and private gardens, custom trellis designs, natural walking paths and a large family loggia.

FRONT ELEVATION

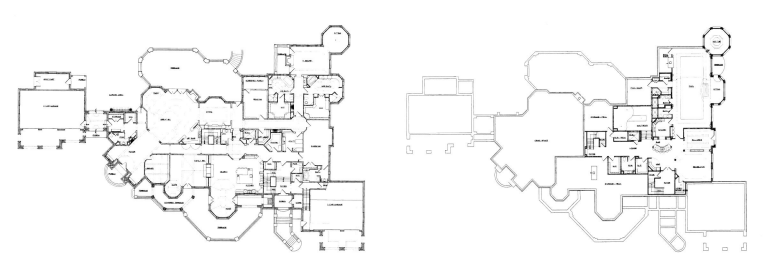

FIRST FLOOR

LOWER LEVEL

129

Moceri Sr. Residence
Oakland Township, Michigan

Project Architect: Jeff Ziegelbaur
Project Designer: Paul Samartino
Builder: Moceri Development
Interior Designer: Fran Murphy

This contemporary estate, integrated into its five-acre site provides panoramic views to the ninth hole of the Wyndgate Golf Course. The 13,000 sq. ft. floor plan continually flows over the site, paying attention to every view possible. The lower level contains more than 9000 sq. ft. of living space, including a theater, full gym, reception area with wet bar and wine tasting rooms. The rear wall of the home is a two-story, butt-glazed glass curtain wall spanning over 80 ft. This element helps the home share space with exterior elements. The crisp interior curves, and the hard horizontal exterior

lines reinforce this classic contemporary estate. The unique material usage includes the mixing of external stone and granite with brick and stucco. The roof lines are highlighted with concrete tiles.

FRONT ELEVATION

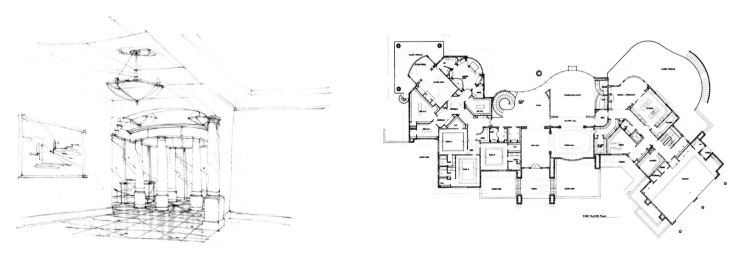

INTERIOR VIEW

FIRST FLOOR PLAN

Adelman Residence
West Bloomfield, Michigan

Project Architect: Jeff Ziegelbaur
Project Designer: Paul Samartino
Builder: Bosco Building Co.
Interior Designer: Lucy Earl

This 19,500 sq. ft. French country manor home
was designed to make the best use of its natural
five-acre surroundings. The home's floor plan
captures important views of natural woodlands and
wetlands, a babbling creek and open meadows.
The low-key entry way and massive fireplaces and
turrets help reinforce its dramatic rustic feeling of
historic European architecture.

REAR ELEVATION

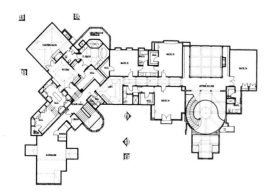

SECOND FLOOR

FIRST FLOOR

Copacia Residence
Oakland Township, Michigan

Project Architect: Jeff Ziegelbaur
Project Designer: Paul Samartino
Builder: Meadow Brook Homes

A Traditional estate design, this home will have an 11,000 sq. ft. formal floor plan, featuring a six-car garage with indoor basketball court. Incorporated into the lower level, which has another 6,000 sq. ft. of entertainment space, are a music room, workout space and arcade.

FRONT ELEVATION

REAR ELEVATION

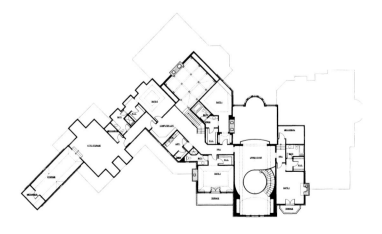

SECOND FLOOR

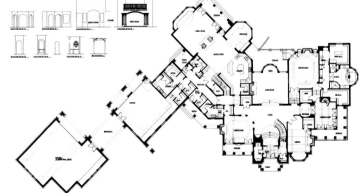

FIRST FLOOR

Henson Residence
Lapeer, Michigan

Project Architect: Randy Hatchard
Project Designer: Paul Samartino

The design of this custom log home will fully integrate it into its one sq. mi. site. The home will set on a peninsula with boat access directly into the house. The main features of this retreat will include a massive, two-story entertaining room, highlighted by a 5,000 gallon fresh water aquarium. The second floor design includes billiards, bar and trophy areas, all of which have overlooking views to the natural surrounding of the site.

REAR ELEVATION

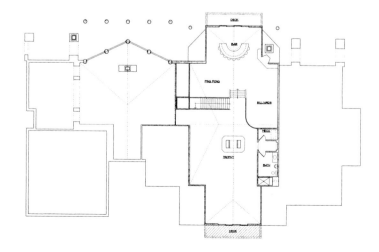

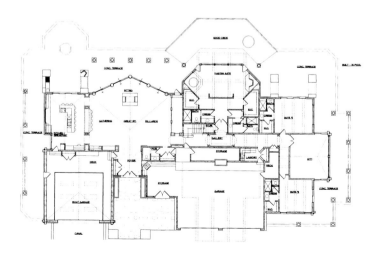

SECOND FLOOR

FIRST FLOOR

Agoston Residence

Turnberry Estates, Novi, Michigan

Project Architect: Jeff Ziegelbaur
Project Designer: Jason Ruthig
Builder: John Richards Homes

This home will have a formal French Eclectic style, exhibiting a formalized room-planning concept. The design will feature a volumetric entrance gallery, solarium and four-car, drive-under garage.

Walloon Cottage

Walloon Lake, Michigan

Project Architect: Randy Hatchard
Project Designer: Jason Ruthig
Builder: Bosco Building Co.

This shingle-style custom cottage is being specially designed for its lakefront site. With both a vast amount of fenestration and strategic room location, the design will allow for pragmatic views from every room.

Burman Residence

Birmingham, Michigan

Project Architect: Randy Hatchard
Project Designer: Jason Ruthig

This narrow in-fill lot supports a French Tudor design. A dramatic entrance foyer and built-in third story recreation area will provide the highlights to this home.

English Manor Estate

Franklin, Michigan

Project Architect: Randy Hatchard
Project Designer: Jason Ruthig
Builder: G. Fisher Construction

The design of this 8,000 sq. ft. English manor estate will accommodate an eight-car attached garage, formal motor court, slate roof, two-story library, 20 ft. x 40 ft. dojo and lower level wine room.

Carollo Residence

Rochester Hills, Michigan

Project Architect: Randy Hatchard
Project Designer: Jason Ruthig
Builder: Custom Homes by Derocher

Extensive brick and stone exterior detailing will bring site-conscious elements to this English Tudor design. The design will center on a sunken entrance foyer and large hearth area, attached to an English conservatory.

Chesterfield Spec

Birmingham, Michigan

Project Architect: Mark Garagiola/Patrick Chianetta
Project Designer: Jason Ruthig

*This Georgian style home is conceptually designed
for a highly visible corner lot. The home as planned
will feature a two-story wraparound covered porch,
authentic dormers and a sculpted third story loft.*

Cunningham Residence (proposed)

Rochester, Michigan

Project Designer: Paul Samartino

*A Traditional Business Estate, this design will boast
over 10,000 sq. ft. of living area, including an
eight-car garage, and a second formal master suite
with a private entrance. Its traditional style will be
reinforced by the strong summitry.*

Demchik Residence

Burce Township, Michigan

Project Designer: Paul Samartino

*The design of this French Italianate villa will
provide dramatic views to a pond and woodlands.
The highlight of the design is a two-story
wine room.*

Franciosi Residence

Birmingham, Michigan

Project Designer: Jason Ruthig

*This authentic two-story French Tudor design
proposes a circular staircase and sitting area, as well
as a rear entry garage and raised master bedroom.
The home is designed for an in-fill site in context
with the surrounding 1920s-era homes.*

Gaynor Residence

Bloomfield Township, Michigan

Project Architect: Jeff Ziegelbaur
Project Designer: Jason Ruthig
Builder: John Richards Homes

*The design of this future lakefront French manor home
is site-conscious, to exhibit a unique motor approach
and dynamic interior space. The concept was to create
a central focal point (octagonal foyer) with intimate
transitions leading to the other formal areas of the design.*

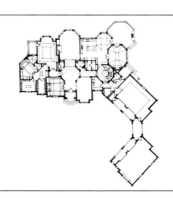

Giftos Residence

Grosse Pointe, Michigan

Project Architect: Jeff Ziegelbaur
Project Designer: Paul Samartino
Builder: Michigan Home Builders

This French traditional home, on an in-fill lot, will be highlighted by a low one-story entrance, which will open to a two-story circular foyer with a reverse staircase. A rear courtyard with pool will bring the living space outdoors.

Gildenberg Residence

West Bloomfield, Michigan

Project Architect: Tim Jahn
Project Designer: Jason Ruthig
Builder: Spartan Homes

This transitional home is being designed for informal living. The project is highlighted with a large built-in pool with volume ceiling and a third story loft with spiral staircase.

Goodison Hills, Model

Rochester, Michigan

Project Architect: Mark Garagiola
Builder: Vito Anthony Homes

A mainstream design with a traditional flare will be the feature of this home.

Griffin Residence (proposed)

Bloomfield Hills, Michigan

Project Designer: Jason Ruthig

This proposed European estate would feature a five-car drive-under garage and carriage house, with extensive exterior detail.

Brookdale Spec Residence

Bloomfield Hills, Michigan

Project Architect: Randy Hatchard
Builder: Kellett Construction

A classic Traditional design with unique detailing and features will be featured in this home.

Kozlowski Residence
Oakland Township, Michigan

Project Architect: Mark Garagiola

A Traditional English Tudor design will set the stage for this Oakland Township home, with extensive masonry detail, customized windows and visually dramatic turrets, and set on a 10-acre parcel.

Labovitz Residence
Birmingham, Michigan

Project Architect: Randy Hatchard
Project Designer: Jason Ruthig
Builder: Derocher Homes

A Bostonian style fill-in project, this 3,500 sq. ft. home will exhibit a prominent vertical facade sculpted with extensive brick and stone detailing.

Le Bear Condominium
Glen Arbor, Michigan

Project Designer: Paul Samartino

This 14-plex condominium on Lake Michigan will exhibit true East Coast Shake style architecture, completed with store accents, cedar shake siding and roof. The design incorporates extensive uses of covered and uncovered porches, which expand living spaces outdoors.

Levey Residence
Bloomfield Hills, Michigan

Project Architect: Jeff Ziegelbaur
Project Designer: Jason Ruthig
Builder: Blair Building

This 8,000 sq. ft. Tudor estate will be designed with a continuous free-flowing floor plan, allowing for panoramic views around the home. It will feature a large private outdoor courtyard, surrounded by a large kitchen, living room and gallery.

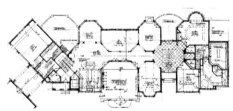

Menuck, A. Residence
Bloomfield Hills, Michigan

Project Architect: Jeff Ziegelbaur
Project Designer: Paul Samartino
Builder: Curtis Building Company

This Colonial Georgian home will overlook a panoramic ravine. The design of this estate will feature an elegant first floor master suite, with carriage house garage and apartment above.

Menuck, Mark Residence

Birmingham, Michigan

Project Architect: Jeff Ziegelbaur
Project Designer: Paul Samartino
Builder: Curtis Building Company

The design of this French Tudor in-fill will include a two-story library, formal dining area and cozy kitchen/family room, and an exterior courtyard. A two-story turret houses a spiral staircase.

Nadhir Residence

Pine Lake, Bloomfield Hills, Michigan

Project Architect: Randy Hatchard
Project Designer: Paul Samartino

This Victorian lakefront home will share panoramic views, thanks to the pie-shaped lot on which it will sit. The main focus of this design is to maximize views while keeping the function of the home in focus. Volume ceilings and lake views will be featured in all of this home's main entertaining spaces.

Pontious Residence

Wolverine Lake, Michigan

Project Architect: Mark Garagiola
Project Designer: Jason Ruthig/Kevin Spell
Builder: M. Rose Construction

This transitional cottage is being designed for a small lakefront lot. The home will feature a large entrance rotunda and a wrap around covered terrace.

Popleton Spec (proposed)

Birmingham, Michigan

Project Architect: Randy Hatchard

A Traditional English design with covered beam porch, English Tudor-style details, and four-car garage, is proposed for this Birmingham home.

Randazzo Residence

Washington Township, Michigan

Project Architect: Jeff Ziegelbaur
Project Designer: Paul Samartino

Fully integrated into its 10-acre site, this 10,000 sq. ft. shingle style home will feature a four-sided design that includes wrap around porches offering 360 degree views of the site. The second floor will be designed into the roof, masking the massive bulk of the home.

Riga Residence
Bloomfield Hills, Michigan

Project Architect: Mark Garagiola
Project Designer: Jason Ruthig
Builder: Wilson Construction

The Traditional European design of this home will feature a large, four-season sunroom, secondary office and raised sitting area off of the master suite.

Samuels Residence
Franklin, Michigan

Project Architect: Mark Garagiola
Project Designer: Jason Ruthig
Builder: Brody Homes

A customized front porch, highlighted by finely detailed wood brackets and planter boxes, will be among the features of this Shingle style home.

Scenic Pines Condos
Bloomfield Hills, Michigan

Project Architect: Jeff Ziegelbaur
Project Designer: Jason Ruthig
Builder: Blair Building Company

This Shingle style ranch home will be detailed with custom wood brackets and metal cupolas.

Schafer Residence
Bloomfield Hills, Michigan

Project Architect: Mark Garagiola
Project Designer: Paul Samartino

This European style ranch home will include over 5,000 sq. ft. of formal living spaces. A drive-under porte-cochere will separate the four-car garage, while a second-floor recording studio with a private entrance will be located under the breezeway.

Schultz Residence (proposed)
West Bloomfield, Michigan

Project Designer: Paul Samartino

A Traditional floor plan, along with a European style elevation, will be the design features of this home. This home will capture views to a creek on its 3/4 acre in-fill site.

Serra Residence
Grand Blanc Township, Michigan

Project Architect: Randy Hatchard
Project Designer: Paul Samartino
Builder: Derocher Construction

With over 4,000 sq. ft. on one floor overlooking a golf course, this Traditional style home will feature formal living spaces along with a drive-under golf cart garage.

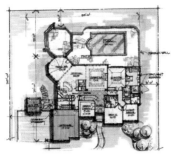

Shapiro Residence (proposed)
Bloomfield Hills, Michigan

Project Designer: Paul Samartino

The design of this estate is inspired by Southern Georgian architecture. This formal home will include a luxurious first floor master suite with formal library. The informal spaces of this home—family room, hearth and kitchen—will be provided with views to a wooded lot.

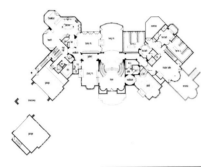

Taube Residence
Lake Angelus, Michigan

Project Architect: Randy Hatchard
Project Designer: Jason Ruthig
Builder: Clark Cobe

This Shingle style lakefront home with a four-car drive under garage will feature a variety of custom details, such as a custom staircase, window seats and eyebrow windows.

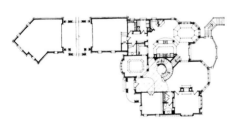

Troutt Residence (proposed)
Traverse City, Michigan

Project Designer: Paul Samartino

This eclectic Traditional estate on Lake Michigan features axial design, which will give it prominent views. The design will feature a raised first floor master suite with a formal master bath and an informal family area, with family room, hearth and kitchen spaces.

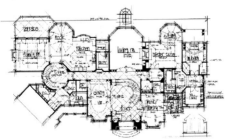

Turtle Lake Spec
Bloomfield Hills, Michigan

Project Designer: Paul Samartino
Builder: John Richards Homes

The design of this spec home will feature traditional European architecture. The design includes a large rotunda foyer with a spiral staircase as a focal point of the home.

Credits

ARCHITECTURAL MODELS
Jon Bell: 128, 131
Zoyes East Inc.: 130

BUILDERS
Abbey Homes: 110 (*23, 25*)
Biltmore Building Company:
   25 (*20*), 32-33, 50, 104 (*8*)
Bingham Development: 30-31
Blair Building Company:
   29 (*27, 29*), 54-55
Blair Building Company/Costello Building:
   29 (*29*), 123-125
Bosco Building Company: 132
CBC Building Company:
   Cover, 16, 24 (*18*), 34-35
Carl Munaco/Paul Carabeli: 38-41
Casadei Homes: 20-21, 112 (*29*)
Cohen Associates: 24 (*16*), 44-49, 115
Clark Cobe: 134
Curtis Building Company:
   25 (*19*), 36-37, 78, 90-91, 106 (*14*)
Curtis/Estate/Wineman—Komer Builders:
   101, 102 (*5*), 106 (*15*), 108 (*19*), 112 (*27, 28, 30*)
Custom Homes by Derocher:
   51, 66-69, 104 (*9, 10*), 110 (*22, 24*)
George Grose Construction: 23
Harb Associates: 22 (*11*)
Huntley Homes: 102 (*3*), 105, 114 (*34*)
Ivanhoe/Huntley Homes: 114 (*32*)
John Richards Homes:
   84-85, 104 (*7*), 107, 108, (*18, 19*)
Moceri Companies: 42-43, 56, 58-65, 86-89,
   106 (*13*), 108 (*17*), 109, 113, 114 (*33*), 130-131
Newcastle Construction: 4, 14, 15, 22 (*12, 13*)
Petrello Builders: 70-73, 111
Saddlebrook Homes: 52-53

BUILDERS (*continued*)
Sal–Mar Homes: 102 (*4*), 103
Singh Homes: 106 (*12*)
Tadian Homes: 11, 74-77
Vito Anthony Homes:
   17-19, 26-27, 102 (*2*), 128-129
Yashinsky Building Company: 24 (*17*), 92-95

ILLUSTRATIONS
AC Illustration: 129, 131,132, 135 (*A*), 137 (*A, B, D, E*),
Dean Chesney Studio: 139 (*D*), 140 (*A, C*), 141 (*B, C, E*),

INTERIOR DESIGNERS
Lucy Earle: 132
DJ Kennedy: 128-129
Fran Murphy: 130-131
Dominick Tringali: 56, 58-65

PHOTOGRAPHY
Scott Benjamin:
   25 (*20*), 38-41, 50, 81-85, 104 (*8*), 116-117,
Christopher Lark: 23,
Glen Calvin Moon: 51
Michael Neumann: Cover, 4, 16, 22, 24 (*17, 18*), 26-27,
   29 (*29*), 33, 36-37, 48-49, 78, 90-95, 98-99, 123-125,
Todd Roberts: 70-73, 111,
Beth Singer: 10-15, 17-22, 24 (*16*), 25 (*19*), 28, 29 (*27*), 30-31,
   34-35, 42-43, 45-47, 52-69, 74-77, 86, 88-89, 96-97,
   100-103, 104 (*7, 9, 10*), 105-110, 112-115

Acknowledgements

For this book, my first venture in documenting all of my work to date, I am indebted to various people I have met throughout my career. These are people who influenced my perspective, allowed me to express my creativity while wisely giving advice and encouragement when needed. Among these people who helped bring this book to fruition are:

My wife and children, who stood by me, allowing me the time needed to put this collection of work together.

My staff of very talented and dedicated designers and architects, all of who have their own unique input into all of our projects.

My long-term colleagues, Randy Hatchard and Jeff Ziegelbaur, whose advice over our 15 years together have helped my homes stand structurally strong and sound. Without their help, we would not be where we are today.

My support staff, who consistently continue to help us excel, and keep the business aspect of running an architectural firm at the highest regard.

And finally, to my wonderful clients. Through them, I have lived my dreams, and through their homes, my dreams will live forever.

Dominick Tringali
2002

To Dominick, "Residential architecture is nothing less than the foundation of society." His humanistic approach not only assures that each home nurtures human life, but that each human life, no matter how young or old, has a part in creating its home.

Architecture is not a mystery when working with Dominick. In sharing each step in the creative process with his clients, he and his staff create a unique involvement with the development of a very intimate lifestyle process…a dream home.

"Residential architecture gives us meaning and purpose. It is what we each call home."

Dominick Tringali

Palazzo Borghese.